CenturyMATHS

FOCUS

Teacher's Support Pack

Year 7/8 Shape and space

Extension

Rita Crust   Charles Cooke

Stanley Thornes (Publishers) Ltd

developed at the Institute of Education,
University of London

**FOCUS TEACHER'S SUPPORT PACK
SHAPE AND SPACE – EXTENSION**
Authors: Rita Crust and Charles Cooke
Illustrator: Angela Lumley

Text © Rita Crust and Charles Cooke
1991
Original illustrations © Stanley Thornes
(Publishers) Ltd 1991

ACKNOWLEDGEMENTS

Professor Celia Hoyles and Dr Richard Noss,
consultants during the development of **Century
Maths**.

**British Library Cataloguing in
Publication Data**

Crust, Rita
   Century maths: Focus teacher's support pack:
   year 7/8 shape and space – extension. –
   (Century maths)
   I. Title   II. Cooke, Charles   III. Series
   510.7

   ISBN 0–7487–1148–1

First published in 1991 by
Stanley Thornes (Publishers) Ltd
Old Station Drive, Leckhampton,
Cheltenham GL53 0DN England

Typeset in Melior and Mixage by
Action Typesetting Ltd, Gloucester
Cover design: Chris Gilbert and
Susie Home
Printed and bound by Martin's of Berwick

Contents

Using the Teacher's Support Packs   1

Problem-solving   3

Keeping the records straight   6

Guide to the completion of Century Maths record sheets   11

Y7/8 Pupil summary page   15

Equipment and materials for Century Maths   16

Flagging of activities in pupils' texts   16

Summary of units   17

1	Symmetry	18
2	Networks	20
3	Congruence	22
4	Polygons	25
5	Making and drawing solids	27
6	Directions	29
7	Enlargement	31
8	Pythagoras' theorem	33
9	Moving points	36
10	Tessellations	38
11	Looking at solids	39

Using the Teacher's Support Packs

Each *Teacher's Support Pack* contains:

- help and information relating to the particular Theme or Focus book;
- guidance on problem solving in the classroom;
- further ideas for problem-solving activities;
- direct links with the National Curriculum Attainment Targets;
- detailed computing support;
- advice on cross-curricular links – both with other subject areas and with the National Curriculum Council's cross-curricular themes.

The *Teacher's Support Packs* include a series of double-page spreads – normally one for each section in the Theme material and one for each unit in the Focus texts. These provide an easy source of reference on your desk.

Theme double-page spreads

Each spread includes:

- Main activities
- Materials required
- Computing references
- Teaching suggestions

- Possible links with National Curriculum Attainment Targets
- Detailed references to Focus texts
- Cross-curricular links.

A 'Summary of sections' page sets out the information above in tabular form. It also indicates the scope for mathematical development in each section.

Focus double-page spreads

Focus double-page spreads are similar to those for the Theme books. Most units in a Focus book have a single related double-page spread in the *Teacher's Support Pack*. The main addition in the Focus spreads is a section of Answers to all numbered questions in the pupils' texts.

Materials required

Any special equipment and materials required are listed on the spreads, with the standard icons used in the pupils' texts to show whether they are essential or merely helpful if they are available. (Equipment and materials listed do not include the standard 'basket' of equipment it is assumed will be available in classrooms at all times – see page 16 of each *Teacher's Support Pack*.)

Computing references

Computing activities are integral to Century Maths. There are two main aspects to the use of the computer:

1 The use of Logo

Century Maths LogoPack 1 is a package of photocopiable activities designed for use by pupils of all abilities. *Logo 2000* provides materials, including software, which make Logo the natural working environment for many of the mathematical problems which teachers and pupils will want to solve. References to both sets of materials appear throughout the pupil texts.

2 Other software packages

References to other software packages are also included in the pupils' materials.

The Logo materials are fully referenced in the double-page spreads for both Theme and Focus material. Some references to other software packages are also included.

Teaching Suggestions

These form the main section in the double-page spreads. They include a general description of the kind of activity to expect. In the Theme spreads they often have a note on the general approach followed by:

- Starting off
- Main activities
- More ideas (when appropriate) and sometimes
- Further activities.

The 'Starting off' section often gives ideas for initial group discussion and ways of organising the groups. The 'More ideas' section may provide comments on extension ideas suggested in the More ideas activities. Related activities are sometimes listed under the 'Further activities' heading.

In the Focus double-page spreads, after a note on the general approach, teaching suggestions are most often set out under unit by unit headings.

Links between Theme and Focus books

The links between Theme and Focus books are set out in the Theme double-page spreads. These Detailed Focus references provide a useful basis for

- planning the follow-up work if you start with a Theme, or
- preparation if you choose to start with the Focus material.

The Focus references indicate the units in the Lead-in (LI), Core (C) and Extension (E) Focus books where related material can be found. These references could be to material which

- would be helpful in working through a Theme;
- would develop skill in the mathematics learned;
- sets the mathematics in another context, enabling the pupil to identify and abstract the mathematics;
- gives further developments which would be of interest to the pupils.

Cross-curricular work

In the Theme *Teacher's Support Packs*, possible links with other subject areas are highlighted, either through links with Attainment Targets or Programmes of Study. These areas are:

- History
- English
- Science
- Geography
- Technology
- NCC cross-curricular themes.

The cross-curricular summary pages offer support and ideas for relevant and constructive cross-curricular work for each Theme.

Problem-solving, record-keeping and assessment

Within the introductory pages you will find a guide to problem solving in the classroom, as well as support and ideas for record-keeping and assessment. (Photocopy masters for record-keeping are provided in the *Worksheet Pack*.)

The range of information and support in the *Teacher's Support Packs* means that they form an integral part of Century Maths for both you and your pupils. They should not be seen merely as answer books or be doomed to collect dust on an inaccessible shelf. They are working documents and are essential support for the pupil materials.

Problem-solving

Why a rationale for problem solving?

Pupils need to experience the application of mathematics in a number of contexts. Opportunities to use mathematical processes should arise from situations meaningful to the learner. Such situations give rise to a number of problems which need to be resolved if a satisfactory solution is to found. However, often the mathematics to be used is not apparent and a great deal of seemingly unnecessary experimentation is undertaken before a solution is reached. The problems encountered may not directly mirror situations met in school but could have common threads of approach. It is the identification of these common threads that enables a pupil to solve a problem.

If pupils are to develop mathematical ability as they grow older, independent thinking needs to be encouraged. This will enable pupils to consider processes by which a problem, or series of problems, can be resolved. These processes may be considered as a series of general strategies that anyone may use in the resolution of a problem. If it is accepted that problem-solving is at the heart of all mathematics, the development of these strategies is crucial for effective mathematical learning.

Some possible general strategies

The notes below relate the strategies to processes involved in developing any Century Maths Theme.

To start with, pupils should be encouraged to *investigate their own problems*. Pupils can be prompted to explore a number of situations and generate their own problems. Mathematical explorations are of value if they do not give rise to the learning of new concepts. Within the context of the chosen situation, ask pupils to:

- list features within the situation that may be considered;

  (Within Century Maths, the *'situation' could be a main activity within a Theme. Discussion with pupils is intended to highlight the features of this activity. From these discussions, pupils could list ideas on which agreement is reached.)*

- list the aspects that *can* be changed and those that *cannot* be changed;

- list the mathematical concepts that may be needed;

  (These points should arise from the group discussions, possibly requiring some teacher guidance from an early stage.)

- try to establish what new concepts – if any – are required;

  (This aspect should evolve naturally from the selected Century Maths Theme through statements such as 'We don't know how to do this . . .' and 'We're stuck!')

- ask 'What would happen if . . .?'

  (This stage occurs when pupil confidence has been established in handling problems observed within any particular Century Maths Theme.)

Getting started

Most situations selected by pupils (and anyone else for that matter!) tend to be rather complicated. Talking through the situation allows a variety of thoughts and ideas to be expressed. This will prompt a variety of questions. These will then become the problems to resolve.

Simplifying the situation

At this stage, it is helpful to try to *simplify the situation* through a series of strategies such as:

- specialising – what will happen in a particular case?

- considering reducing
  - the size of the variables (take the simplest case), or
  - the number of variables in use at any one time;
- modelling – making a few assumptions that help to start resolving the problem;
- organising the approach to be taken – random trial and improvement may lead to blind alleys. To avoid these, consider
  - trial and improvement methods;
  - systematic listing of all possiblities;
  - dealing with one variable at a time while holding the others constant.

(Note, however, that blind alleys can often prove to be a rich vein for extending mathematical knowledge even though they may not advance the solution to the problem in hand.)

Representing and recording information

Most people – and that includes pupils – find great difficulty in expressing themselves succinctly when using words and numbers. However, the key to a sound resolution of any situation is the ability to *represent and record information* in such a way that it can be clearly understood and be or benefit to anyone requiring it. To this end, a good diagram or notation is often the key to the successful solution of a problem. Methods of recording information will include:

- informal diagrams and notation;
- pictures and diagrams used to *describe* things clearly;
- tables, graphs, etc. used to *reveal any relationships* within information;
- tables, tree diagrams, matrices, etc. used to *classify* information.

The emphasis should be on *when* to use such representations rather than *how* to use them.

Conjectures and generalisations

At some stage, pupils will start saying they have 'found things out'. This elementary statement is the beginning of their *making and testing conjectures and generalisations*. Within this stage, pupils will have to consider a number of processes, including:

- spotting patterns and relationships of different kinds;
- checking and testing them on further cases;
- trying to find reasons for them;
- making generalisations from particular cases;
- trying to verify the generalisation for all cases;
- moving from number into algebra;
- extending the notation.

Passing through these stages, pupils may feel confident that they have resolved à certain situation and have a sound argument to present. But the most important stage within the problem-solving process is yet to come.

Explaining to others

Can the outcome arrived at be *explained to others* in such a way that they are *convinced* that the solution is sound? For such a *communication to be valid*, pupils may have to use instructions, diagrams, etc, using oral, written or pictorial methods, including technological means.

Having presented the arguments to others, has the pupil *proved* that the solution is sound? This final stage allows others to question and criticise any arguments heard. This affords the presenter the opportunity of having a rudimentary analysis carried out in a friendly environment.

Problem solving within Century Maths

As an aid to pupils acquiring problem-solving strategies, a selection of problem-solving activities is built into the *Teacher's Support Packs*. Some of the activities selected are taken from the Theme/Focus material and extended to include illustrations on how to develop a number of the strategies listed above. In this way, teachers are able to observe how Century Maths supports these strategic skills.

From its inception, Century Maths has been developed from a problem-solving standpoint. In both Theme and Focus books Century Maths provides many opportunities to use and develop problem-solving skills. The situations provided will act as a springboard for the pupils to consider further situations. These new situations will, in turn, give rise to many problems requiring resolution.

Keeping the records straight

What do we need to record?

How does the pupil's work fit into the record?

Record-keeping needs to be a constructive activity. How can we achieve this?

Who are we keeping the record for?

How can I find the time to produce all these records?

How often should the recording be done?

Can the pupils take more responsibility for keeping records?

Keeping a record of progress and achievement for each pupil is a central area of teacher assessment. Without a sound record-keeping mechanism, capable of providing evidence to substantiate a teacher's professional judgment, the assessment of each pupil will lose credibility. However, there is no one correct way to achieve this – each school has unique requirements, and every teacher must have a clear understanding of the aims behind any agreed system adopted by the school. Such a system must be:

- unobtrusive within the teaching environment;
- seen by pupils and teachers alike to be a positive activity;
- easily manageable for the teacher and not a time-consuming exercise.

Record-keeping within Century Maths attempts to satisfy these three major criteria. Essentially, each pupil is given a simple four-part assessment record, which he or she completes regularly. The teacher adds comments and suggestions to this. The four parts of the assessment record are the Record of Achievement, the Action Report, the Review and the Summary (see pages 11–14).

In order to illustrate fully how Century Maths record-keeping satisfies the three criteria stated, the questions posed at the beginning of this section are answered in detail below.

What do we need to record?

Century Maths recording concentrates on observable evidence, gained from the classroom situation. It contains a pupil's initial reactions to the Theme material (see Record of Achievement, page 11). This is then followed up with on-going pupil comments relating to daily/weekly progess with notes referring to allied Focus materials used (see Action report). The teacher makes comments at regular intervals on the Record of Achievement, having negotiated with the pupil what will be written down. Such comments may include specific references to some areas of mathematics handled successfully or with difficulty, as well as more general comments.

How does the pupil's work fit into the record?

At the end of each Theme, pupils complete the sections on the Review relating to their feelings about the work on Theme and Focus materials and how they think they have progressed. Teachers will then make a summative statement about the pupils' work during the Theme on the Summary, possibly using pupils' work as substantiation of the comments made.

Record-keeping needs to be a constructive activity. How can we achieve this?

This is achieved in Century Maths by providing a method of record-keeping which:

- is flexible;

- is easy to use;
- is meaningful to the pupils and teachers;
- acknowledges the activities which pupils have been involved in – and not only those within the context of the National Curriculum;
- contains evidence of work produced by the pupils;
- is integrated into the work being carried out;
- provides a method of supplying cross-curricular evidence;
- involves discussion between pupils and teachers.

Who are we keeping the record for?

- The pupils: to give a sense of ownership of their work as well as ensuring a sense of progress;
- the teacher: to assist in planning and to inform about the success (or otherwise) of a teaching strategy, while at the same time, through regular communication with the pupils, increasing the teacher's knowledge of each pupil;
- the next teacher;
- the pupil's parents;
- the head teacher and the governing body;
- whoever is monitoring the National Curriculum.

How can I find the time to produce all these records?

Century Maths record-keeping is an integral part of the classroom environment. It merges into the teacher's observation of and interaction with the pupil in the classroom. It supports the learning and teaching, facilitates pupil progress and continuity, but does not encroach upon the activities in hand.

Can the pupils take more responsibility for keeping records?

Clearly, the Century Maths model of record-keeping places pupil involvement at the very heart of the activity. All records are 'pupil-driven' with the teacher monitoring and commenting when appropriate. Assessment is from both parties, with pupil comments relating to their own feelings about the progress being achieved, as well as teacher comments relating to a variety of activities observed.

How often should the recording be done?

The record can be filled in by teachers as and when they deem it necessary, but generally about once a week. The most appropriate time for teachers to talk to the pupils about their comments is when both parties feel it would be most beneficial.

But ... I think I need a checklist to keep me up to date with each of my pupils.

Although Century Maths does not subscribe to a checklist mode of record-keeping, perhaps some schools or departments may require such a list as part of the overall assessment procedure. Teachers could develop a checklist based on the Focus coverage indicated within the pupil records. It could serve to:

- build up an overview related to the attainment targets (but this should be only one reason for keeping records);

- indicate where the 'gaps' are appearing in coverage of Focus material;

- show the 'spread' of levels being tackled by each pupil. A possible model for such a checklist is provided (see Pupil summary page).

However, you should be aware that such a checklist:

- indicates coverage and not necessarily achievement;

- is not evidence of a pupil's progress, merely an indication of what was observed on a particular day;

- may give the false impression that you are only interested in National Curriculum attainment targets.

Fine, but why has Century Maths developed its record-keeping and assessment around the pupils?

There are many reasons why we have decided to do this, some more important than others. Some of our reasons you may disagree with. We consider that pupil involvement in record-keeping:

- encourages pupils to have a sense of ownership over their own work;

- increases pupils' awareness of the very nature of mathematics;

- allows pupils to observe and understand their progress and the continuity within Century Maths;

- heightens pupils' awareness of their own achievements and development;

- develops pupils' understanding of where their mathematics fits within a cross-curricular framework;

- enables pupils to identify their own strengths and weaknesses;

- develops pupils' reflective and analytical skills.

This list not in order of priority, nor is it exhaustive, but it does indiate a firm belief in an active role for all pupils in their own assessment.

Do we always have to base our judgments on written evidence?

Teachers are the best people to assess their own pupils. They will be aware of what guidance has been given and how pupils have responded to a variety of situations. This essential information forms the central part of any assessment and can be gleaned from observation, discussion and questioning, or any other interaction, including a written response.

But how can we assess an individual's input within a group situation?

Here, many general strategies are available. It is important to select suitable strategies for providing the most useful and reliable evidence, without distorting the task in hand. Consider:

- general observation of the group dynamics;
- discussion with the whole group as a natural part of the activity;
- discussion with individuals during and after the task;
- individually-completed written reports;
- group evaluations of each person's involvement and input.

Through the Century maths record sheets, the individual pupils' involvement within any group activity should become more apparent.

And how can we assess the application of their mathematics effectively?

The application of mathematics underpins all the attainment targets. It represents essential aspects of *all* mathematical activities. It is, therefore, not desirable to assess this separately. However, if you consider the assessment of the application of mathematics appropriate, you should focus on three essential strands of pupils' mathematical development, allowing a possible fourth strand (extension) for differentiation at the higher levels.

These three strands are:

- task management
- communication
- mathematical insight.

Under these three strands (or four with the extension strand added) a criteria matrix can be created.

Such a matrix should be used bearing in mind the teacher's knowledge of the pupils and the way the pupils have worked. This is essential if effective assessment is to take place.

One example of a criteria matrix is given overleaf. When using such a grid, a number of questions must be addressed:

- is 'observed once' sufficient evidence to record a pupil's progress in terms of a level descriptor?
- What method do we adopt to moderate a pupil's work seen to be at different levels for different strands of the matrix?
- What role does the 'Extension' column play – if any – in the overall assessment of a pupil's work?

Having considered these and many other questions, we hope that the matrix will be some assistance when you come to consider each activity to be assessed within the Theme material.

Criteria Matrix for the Application of Mathematics

Level	Task Management	Mathematical Insight	Communication	Extension
3	Select materials and mathematics	Offer evidence of understanding Check results	Explain work in clear manner	Make and test some simple predictions
4	Select appropriate materials from given resources Show evidence of methodical planning	Test patterns observed	Use appropriate method to record results	Use examples to test statements
5	Make request for the appropriate materials Plan for full information	Check patterns and calculations Suggest possible outcomes	Interpret the given information	Make and test statements relating to the task in hand
6	Design a task and select appropriate equipment and mathematics Obtain all required information	Record and test findings with accuracy Show evidence of 'trial and improvement' methods	Present findings in oral, written or visual form	Make and test generalisations and hypotheses
7	Devise a mathematical task Decide upon an agreed structure	Work methodically within the agreed structure Use 'trial and improvement' methods Follow a chain of mathematical reasoning, spotting inconsistencies	Review progress and present findings in an appropriate manner	Follow new investigation using some alternative approaches
8	Devise a mathematical task Make a detailed plan of the work	Work methodically through the task Check information for completeness Consider the results in the light of the original task	Present findings in a coherent manner State evidence of reasons for making chosen decisions	Conjecturise using such statements as: 'If . . . then . . .' define, reason, prove and disprove
9	Design and plan a mathematical task	Consider and state conjectures and show whether true, false or not proven. Evidence of the use of counter examples Reach a successful conclusion	Be able to define and reason through the task Interpret findings clearly	Use symbolisation Recognise and use 'necessary and sufficient' condition
10	Design and plan a mathematical task	Use symbolisation with confidence Reach a successful conclusion	Present alternative solutions Justify with evidence the route selected	Give definitions which are sufficient or minimal Construct a proof by contradiction

Guide to the completion of Century Maths record sheets

Record of achievement

Name:

Class:

Theme/Focus:

Start date:

Main activity

A simple description of what the pupil intends to do, which could be explained better later in the project

First ideas

What we are going to do?

'Brainstorming' kind of response after discussion in a whole class group and smaller group

Theme / Focus

On-going opportunity to record Focus maths links

Other activities

To be added to as the Theme develops

T

Suggestions by teacher, helpful notes, positive comments

Action report

Name:

Class:

Theme/Focus:

Finishing date:

Week	What we achieved	Theme / Focus	Theme / Focus	Comment How is your work progressing? Any major problems? Are you enjoying the Theme/Focus materials? What would you like help with?
1	*Factual record of what has been completed or started*	*Note made of linked Focus Work*	*Note made of computer work*	*On-going self-assessment and evaluation, with the statements made being a helpful guide for discussion between pupil and teacher the following week*
2				
3				
4				
5				
6				

12

Review – Looking back . . .

Theme/Focus: 🧩 Theme / Focus

Week 1 2 3 4 5 6

Are you pleased with your work on the Theme/Focus materials? Which parts went well?

Positive achievements

Group members:

Note of who has been working with the pupil

How well did you work together?

Co-operative skills tackled

What have you learned during your work on the Theme/Focus materials?

Hopefully, statements relating to Attainment Target 1 might emerge

Which parts of the Theme/Focus materials did you not enjoy?

Negative aspects opened up so that the teacher can talk these through

🖥 How did your computer work go?

Importance of information technology skills stressed

Which maths caused you some difficulty?

Targets for the future

How could you have improved your work?

Targets for the future

🧩 Which maths links did you do?

Connections with Focus units

Summary

CenturyMaths

Name:

Class:

Theme/Focus:

Date:

Theme ⟷ Focus (puzzle pieces)

Main activities

Theme:

Summary by pupil

Focus:

Achievements

National Curriculum Attainment Targets
covered/levels attained/
areas of mathematics involved

*Some sort of teacher assessment
or simply work covered*

Pupil comment:

Opportunies for improved communication between pupils, teachers and parents

Teacher comment:

Opportunities for improved communication between pupils, teachers and parents

Parent comment:

Opportunities for improved communication between pupils, teachers and parents

Year 7/8 Pupil summary page

Name:

Class:

Handling data

Units

	1	2	3	4	5	6	7	8	9	10	11			
Lead-in	1	2	3	4	5	6	7	8	9	10	11			
Core	1	2	3	4	5	6	7	8	9	10	11			
Extension	1	2	3	4	5	6	7	8	9	10	11	12	13	14

Number

Units

	1	2	3	4	5	6	7	8	9	10	11	12
Lead-in	1	2	3	4	5	6	7					
Core	1	2	3	4	5	6	7	8	9	10	11	12
Extension	1	2	3	4	5	6	7	8	9	10	11	12

Shape and space

Units

	1	2	3	4	5	6	7	8	9	10	11
Lead-in	1	2	3	4	5	6	7				
Core	1	2	3	4	5	6	7	8	9	10	
Extension	1	2	3	4	5	6	7	8	9	10	11

Algebra

Units

	1	2	3	4	5	6	7	8	9	10	11	12	13	14	15
Lead-in	1	2	3	4	5	6	7	8	9	10	11				
Core	1	2	3	4	5	6	7	8	9	10	11	12			
Extension	1	2	3	4	5	6	7	8	9						

Theme

Animals · Trees · Neighbourhood · School fair · Festivals · Ourselves · Patterns · Traffic · Holidays · Connections · Music · Food

At the end of each half term, shade in Themes and Focus units you have worked on.

Equipment and materials for Century Maths

The basket of equipment

 This 'basket' contains all the general equipment and materials we would expect to be available in the classroom at all times for working on **Century Maths**:

calculators	sellotape
compasses	staplers
felt tips	plain paper
glue sticks	graph paper
pencils	1 cm square and
protractors	1 cm isometric grid paper
rubbers	1 cm square and
rulers	1 cm isometric dotty paper
scissors	tracing paper

More specific equipment and materials, required for a particular task in a Theme section or Focus unit, are shown on the relevant spreads in the pupil books and the *Teachers's Support Packs*. These fall into two categories:

✔ equipment and materials that you *will* need

○ equipment and materials that you *may* need

Flagging of activities in pupils' texts

Theme books

☐ highlights key activity(ies) on page

● supplementary activity(ies), often optional, or series of stages in an activity

▶ more ideas based on the same topic

Focus books

■ a pupil activity

☐ activity with pupil-generated answer – no answer/solution given in *Teacher's Support Pack*

 activity for which answer/solution is given in *Teacher's Support Pack*

Y 7/8 Shape and Space – Extension: summary of units

Unit titles	Activities	Materials required	NC NATs (PoS) Levels	Teacher's notes on scope for maths development
1 **Symmetry** Pages 2 – 11	Looking at symmetries of a variety of shapes	○ ▣ Small mirrors	**NAT 4** 5c; 6b, f, g	
2 **Networks** Pages 12 – 19	Investigations on networks		**NAT 4** 5d	
3 **Congruence** Pages 20 – 27	Problem-solving tasks relating to congruence	✔ ▤ 1 Sets of pentominoes 8 × 8 square board		
4 **Polygons** Pages 28 – 35	Extending knowledge of angles and polygons through spatial puzzles	✔ ▤ 2, 3, 4, 5 ▣	**NAT 4** 5b; 6e, f	
5 **Making and drawing solids** Pages 36 – 43	Activities relating to isometric drawing and solid models	✔ Centicubes ○ Polydron ▣	**NAT 4** 6a	
6 **Directions** Pages 44 – 51	Activities relating to use of bearings and coordinates		**NAT 4** 5e; 6h; 7a	
7 **Enlargement** Pages 52 – 59	Tasks involving the concepts scale factor and similarity	▣		
8 **Pythagoras' theorem** Pages 60 – 71	Activities and questions relating to Pythagoras' theorem	▣	**NAT 2** 6g **NAT 4** 4g; 7c	
9 **Moving points** Pages 72 – 83	Activities relating to curves and use of linkages	✔ Geostrips and paper fasteners or drinking straws and pipecleaners or card strips, a hole punch and poppers String Drawing pins Small objects such as blocks Counters ▣	**NAT 4** 7b	
10 **Tessellations** Pages 84 – 89	Investigations on the properties of polygons and the congruence of shapes	✔ ▤ 6 Square and rectangular tiles ○ ATM Tiles Acetate sheet and OHP ▣	**NAT 4** 4b; 6e	
11 **Looking at solids** Pages 90 – 95	Function work extending areas covered in Unit 5	▣	**NAT 4** 6a	

Unit 1 Symmetry

Activities

A symmetry puzzle	page 2
Another symmetry puzzle!	page 3
Spirolaterals	pages 4–5
Islamic patterns	pages 6–9
Wheel trim designs	page 10
Making your own designs	pages 11–12

Materials required

Islamic patterns

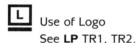 Small mirrors

Computing references

A symmetry puzzle

L Use of Logo
See **LP** TR1, TR2.

Spirolaterals

L Use of Logo

Links with National Curriculum Attainment Targets: Programmes of Study level descriptors

NAT	Level	PoS Descriptor(s)
4	5	c
	6	b, f, g

Teaching suggestions

This unit aims to provide opportunities for pupils to acquire further knowledge and skills relating to the symmetries of a variety of shapes within a practical problem-solving environment, incorporating the use of the computer when appropriate.

Although some pupils may work through this unit as individuals, there is much to be gained from small group work and pupil–pupil discussion as well as teacher–pupil discussion about the issues which arise.

A symmetry puzzle and Another symmetry puzzle!

In both these activities, a pupil's intuitive immediate response to question 1 is likely to be based upon an assumption that the fold line is vertical. Question 2 is designed to encourage pupils to rethink their previous response and realise that any of the four sides could be the fold line. In question 3, choosing each of the four sides gives a different initial shape. Pupils could describe their final shapes as quadrilaterals, pentagons or hexagons and compare the dimensions with the original shape.

A full discussion of this first example, accompanied by appropriate practical work, will pay dividends as the task develops. The need for a systematic approach should be emphasised.

Spirolaterals

Pupils will need to work accurately and methodically through this task. As they investigate the shapes they produce, they may notice that: three digit spirolaterals such as (1, 2, 3) have rotational symmetry; (3, 2, 1) is a reflection of (1, 2, 3); (2, 3, 2) has lines of symmetry as well as rotational symmetry.

Drawing spirolaterals using Logo and producing screen dumps makes the task much more enjoyable. Using Logo enhances the possibility of investigating four and five digit spirolaterals. Do they return to their starting point or do they walk off the page? Spirolaterals in which the angle of turn is 60^0 can be investigated using isometric grid paper but angles of any size can be turned using Logo.

Islamic patterns

This practical task aims to show pupils that simple shapes reflected in more than one mirror can produce quite complex designs which have symmetry. They are then encouraged to look in their own environment for similar designs.

. . . Symmetry

Wheel trim designs

This activity provides a further everyday situation where pupils are encouraged to look at familiar objects which have symmetry.

Making your own designs

This practical task leads pupils through the stages of drawing a symmetrical design.

Answers

Page 2

1
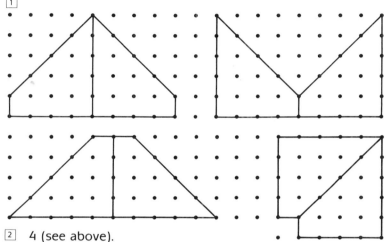

2 4 (see above).

3 By using a mirror to check other possible positions.

Page 3

1
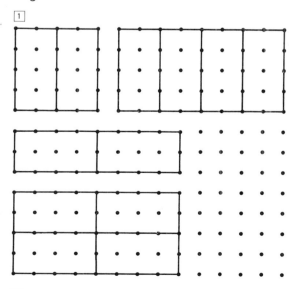

2 2 (see above).

3 Check by using a mirror.

Page 4

1 [FD 1 RT 90 FD 2 RT 90 FD 3 RT 90] Repeat 4 times.

2 Rotational symmetry order 4.

3 It is a reflection of (1, 2, 3).

4 Rotational symmetry order 4.

5 Line and rotational symmetry.

6 Blade sizes; area of blades; some are rectangles; some are windmills.

Page 5

7 [FD 2 RT 60 FD 3 RT 60] Repeat 3 times.

8 Line symmetry.

9 Same dimensions and shapes. It involves a rotation and translation.

Activities

A network problem	page 12
A story network	page 13
Euler's walkabout	pages 13–15
Analysing networks	page 16
The travelling salesman's problem	page 17
More travel problems	page 18
Adding on polygons	page 19

Materials required

▢ Computing references

Links with National Curriculum Attainment Targets: Programmes of Study level descriptors

NAT	Level	PoS Descriptor(s)
4	5	d

Teaching suggestions

The topic of networks, more correctly called Graph Theory, is rich in providing material for investigations. In these activities, pupils may make conjectures and test them by designing their own examples.

The tasks do not require extensive knowledge of other branches of mathematics but do require insight, visual ability and heuristic skills which are all regarded as being at the heart of 'doing' mathematics.

A network problem

Shongo networks can give rise to interesting number work which will be dealt with in Y9 Shape and Space.

Euler's walkabout and Analysing networks

In this activity, pupils could investigate town plans of other cities, such as Venice, New York, Paris and Nuremberg, which have islands and bridges.

In the activity, the problem of what conditions are necessary and sufficient for a network to be traversible is completely solved:

● If there are no vertices of odd degree, the network is traversible: the drawing can start at any vertex, and will finish there.

● If there are exactly two vertices of odd degree, the network is semi-traversible: one of these vertices is the start and the other the finish of the drawing.

● If there are more than two vertices of odd degree, the network is non-traversible.

Pupils could investigate the numbers of vertices of odd and even degrees for a variety of networks, and make the conjecture that the number of vertices of odd degree is always even.

The travelling salesman's problem

There is no similar test which can be used to decide if a network has a travelling salesman's route.

. . . **Networks**

Adding on polygons

The rule for patterns of polygons is:
If R is the number of regions (including the exterior region), E is the number of edges and V is the number of vertices in a network of polygons drawn in the plane, then
$R - E + V = 2$.

This result is similar to the result for polyhedra known as Euler's Theorem:
R is replaced by F, the number of faces of the polyhedron.
We make the connection between these results in Y 9 Shape and Space.

Interesting material on networks can be found in the books of mathematical pastimes by Martin Gardner.

The historical development of the topic is treated in N.L. Biggs, E.K. Lloyd and R.J. Wilson, *Graph Theory 1736–1936*, Oxford, 1976; this includes a translation of Euler's paper on the bridges of Koeningsberg, and a description of Hamilton's game.

Answers

Page 17

1. Yes
2. 0 or 2 odd nodes gives a traversible network.
3. No   4. No   5. No
6. Yes   7. Yes   8. Yes

Page 18

1. If A → B and B → C is equidistant, then pupils may suggest either B or C.
2. Answers will vary as D comes closer.
3. Not really – 10 people have a significant distance to travel.

Unit **3** # Congruence

Activities

Congruent keys   page 20

Polyominoes   page 21

Pentomino rectangles   page 22

Pentomino puzzles   page 23

The pentomino game   page 24

Hexomino puzzles   page 25

Two halves make a whole   pages 26–27

Materials required

Pentomino rectangles, Pentomino puzzles and The pentomino game

 Sets of pentominoes if possible made from different coloured cardboard
8 x 8 square boards

Two halves make a whole

  1

☐ Computing references

Links with National Curriculum Attainment Targets: Programmes of Study level descriptors

Teaching suggestions

This unit aims to provide a variety of practical problem-solving tasks which motivate pupils' interest in the concept of congruence because they see its relevance to their everyday lives, or because it can help them to solve a puzzle or win a game.

Although some pupils may benefit from working through some of these tasks on their own, many of the activities are more appropriate for small group work and opportunity for both pupil – pupil and teacher – pupil discussion should be provided. Discussion of whether one polyomino is 'different' from another can lead to a deeper understanding of congruence.

Congruent keys

This task provides an everyday situation in which it may be vital to identify objects which are exactly the same shape and size. But when are two keys congruent? In what ways are the keys different?

This activity provides an excellent opportunity for discussion, classification and accurate recording of the features of each key as a means of identifying those which are congruent.

Polyominoes

It is essential to provide some practical materials to support this activity. Although squares of card may be the most obvious resource to use, there are advantages in using interlocking cubes. These must be linked so that they lie flat on a surface. The shapes created using interlocking cubes can be moved around easily when pupils are trying to decide whether two shapes really are congruent or whether they are merely different orientations of the same shape.

The purpose of this activity is to provide an opportunity for pupils to explore within mathematics itself, to develop their ability to work systematically and to organise their findings. Pupils need to record their findings diagrammatically on squared paper. They also need to be able to identify congruent shapes.

One way of tackling this problem is as follows:

However many squares (cubes) we have, we can always place them in a straight line. This should be recorded diagrammatically on squared paper. We can then remove one square and attach it in various positions alongside the remaining row of squares. Again this should be recorded diagrammatically on squared paper.

However, some of the shapes may be congruent. Repetitions of the same shape should be deleted. A second square should be removed from the original row . . .

The criterion of success in this task, and the other tasks in this unit, is not that pupils should obtain the right answer, but that they should approach the work systematically, record their findings and be able to explain what they have done.

Pentomino rectangles

This activity benefits from several pupils working with a set of pentominoes each, and sharing their ideas and the challenge. It is worth making several sets of pentominoes (each from different coloured cardboard to help with sorting).

Alternatively, the familiar investigation of asking pupils to make their own set of pentominoes could precede this activity.

Pupils should be allowed to explore making their own shapes with the pentominoes before settling down to searching for rectangles.

Points to note

If some pupils find the challenge rather tough, allow them to use the same pentomino twice inside the same rectangle.

Pupils may make rectangles which are swaps of ones already made (possibly reflected and/or rotated). This may need some discussion. The rectangles all have an area that is a multiple of five.

Examples

There are many possible rectangles. Here are some simple examples:

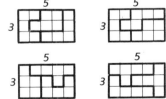

. . . **Congruence**

Note that the 'U' and 'P' shapes are very useful.

Here are more rectangles using up to 12 different pentominoes.

Answers

Page 21

1.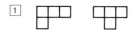

2. 12: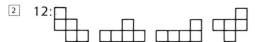

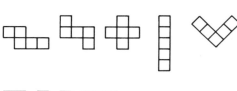

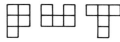

3. 35. Here are 12 hexominoes:

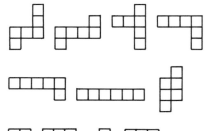

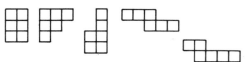

Here are two possible five by six rectangles, using all 12 pentominoes. Pupils can be asked to find the areas of each rectangle. It is interesting to see how they do this.

Further activities

There are many published puzzles concerning pentominoes.

Unit 4 Polygons

Activities

Polygons	page 28
Random quadrilaterals	page 29
Skydiving	page 30
Skydiver rings	page 31
Can you square it?	page 32
Tangrams	page 33
Angles in triangles	page 34
Angles in polygons	page 35

Materials required

Random quadrilaterals

  2

Skydiver rings

  3

Can you square it?

  4, 5

Computing references

Random quadrilaterals

L Use of QUAD procedure to draw quadrilaterals

Links with National Curriculum Attainment Targets: Programmes of Study level descriptors

NAT	Level	PoS Descriptor(s)
4	5	b
	6	e, f

Teaching suggestions

This unit provides opportunities for pupils to consolidate and extend their knowledge about angles and polygons within situations which present them with spatial puzzles to solve. In order to solve these puzzles they will need to work methodically, record their findings, use trial and improvement methods as well as making and testing simple hypotheses.

Although some pupils may benefit from working through some of these tasks on their own, many of the activities are more appropriate for small group work, and opportunity for both pupil–pupil and teacher–pupil discussion should be provided.

Polygons

This introductory activity is intended to enable pupils to recall work previously covered. The context provided is one in which they make a variety of polygons and then name and write about their own shapes.

Random quadrilaterals

In this activity, the computer generates quadrilaterals and pupils name and identify their properties.

Skydiving and Skydiver rings

This activity provides a real-life situation for pupils to discuss and experiment with, in which the properties of polygons are relevant.

Can you square it?

This puzzle situation encourages pupils to cut and reorganise the pieces of one shape in order to make a different shape. Trial and error alone is unlikely to be rewarding. Pupils need to think clearly about what they are trying to do: they need to consider the lengths and angles of the shapes they begin with and what they want to end with.

Tangrams

In this activity, pupils will discover that it really is amazing what shapes you can produce, using a few simple shapes and rearranging them in all possible ways!

Angles in triangles and Angles in polygons

These tasks focus on finding the sum of the angles in a polygon based on a practical activity: the notion of walking around a polygon and determining through what angle you have turned.

. . . **Polygons**

Answers

Page 29

Due to the randomising within the Logo procedure, questions 1 to 4 can produce a variety of different answers.

Here is a set of typical results, produced by using **QUAD** ten consecutive times.

Note:
When the picture has been too large for the screen, that particular result has been ignored.

Shape	Symmetry	Description	Sides
Kite	1 line	2 pairs of equal sides 1 pair of equal angles	No
Quadrilateral	No	No	No
Trapezium	No	No	1 pair of opposite
Isosceles trapezium	1 line	1 pair of equal sides 2 pairs of equal angles	1 pair of opposite
Quadrilateral	No	No	No
Parallelogram	Rotational – order 2	Opposite sides and angles equal	2 pairs of opposite
Square	4 lines Rotational – order 4	All sides equal All angles equal	2 pairs of opposite
Trapezium	No	No	1 pair of opposite
Quadrilateral	No	No	No
Rectangle	2 lines Rotational – order 2	Opposite sides equal All angles equal	2 pairs of opposite

Page 31

1. The first. It is a stronger network.
2. Rings which have rotational symmetry are more stable.

Page 34

1. $360°$
2. $x + y + z = 360°$
3. $180°$
4. $x + a + y + b + z + c = 540°$

Page 35

1. $540°$

Activities

Isometric drawing	pages 36–38
How many cubes?	page 39
Plans and elevations	pages 40–41
Making solids from nets	pages 42–43

Materials required

Isometric drawing

 Centicubes

Making solids from nets

 Polydron

⬜ Computing references

Isometric drawing

 Possible use of Microworld 'Isogrid'

Links with National Curriculum Attainment Targets: Programmes of Study level descriptors

NAT	Level	PoS Descriptor(s)
4	6	*a*

Unit 5 Making and drawing solids

Teaching suggestions

Isometric drawing and How many cubes?

The skills to be developed in these activities are: producing an isometric drawing from a solid model; constructing a solid model from an isometric drawing; identifying isometric drawings from different viewpoints.

Plans and elevations

There may be some discrepancies if we regard a plan as a 'bird's eye view' of a building as seen from above or as the ground floor plan. This could be brought out in discussion.

Making solids from nets

There are 35 'different' hexominoes. Ideas of congruence (fitting exactly on) are important here. Discussion can focus on what is meant in this instance by 'different'. We would consider two hexominoes to be the same if one can be turned around (rotated) or turned over (reflected) so that it is congruent with the other.

We would expect two types of hexomino to be rejected as impossible nets – those which have five squares 'in a row' and those which have four squares 'around a point'. The reasons for this should be made clear. This is a simple introduction to the idea of proof: 'this cannot work because of . . .'

The hexominoes which are nets of a cube can be obtained as a subset of the total set by testing each one in turn.

Other methods are to use a cube whose faces can be separated. The kit Polydron, available at Early Learning Centres, can be used. Pupils start with a cube and 'unzip' it until it lies flat. They can also use the idea of a Schlegel diagram ⬚ .

This is a 'flattened' drawing of a 'topless' cube. So they add on a square to represent the top and cut along the edges as required to produce a net. One has to imagine that distorted squares become real squares when this is done.

Further activities

Similar tasks can be set using equilateral triangles instead of squares. The net of a tetrahedron will use four triangles, that of an octahedron eight triangles: there are 11 different nets for the octahedron.

Games for two can be developed using hexominoes or pentominoes. What size of paper will you need in order to cut out all the nets of a cube? The game could involve placing the nets on the board so that ultimately an opponent cannot place a net without overlapping others. Pupils can alter the rules by agreement.

. . . Making and drawing solids

Answers

Page 38

1. The middle drawing is made from the same 2 solid shapes.

Page 39

1. (Top left) 62; (top right) 59; (middle left) 31(29); (middle right) 22; (bottom left) 52; (bottom right) 18(17, 19)
2. 30; 20; 11; 8; 24; 12
3. Yes – see numbers for middle left and bottom right buildings in 1.
4. Discuss the number of cubes in each of the pupils' models with them.

Page 43

1. (left) 3 hidden; (right) 3 hidden
2. (left) 8; (right) 12
3. (left) 8, 18; (right) 12, 24

Unit **6 Directions**

Activities

Bearings   pages 44–45

Rescued from the sea   pages 46–47

Bird island   pages 48–49

3-D coordinates   page 50

3-D noughts and crosses   page 51

Materials required

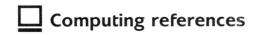 Computing references

Links with National Curriculum Attainment Targets: Programmes of Study level descriptors

NAT	Level	PoS Descriptor(s)
4	5	e
	6	h
	7	a

Teaching suggestions

This unit aims to ensure that pupils acquire concepts and skills relating to the use of bearings to define direction in two-dimensional space as well as the specification of location in two- or three-dimensional space, using coordinates.

It is intended that the situations provided will enable these concepts and skills to be acquired within contexts which pupils perceive to be interesting and relevant.

Although pupils will benefit from working through some of these tasks on their own, some of the activities involving discussion and collaboration are appropriate for small group work. Opportunity for both pupil–pupil and teacher–pupil discussion should be provided.

Bearings

These tasks provide an opportunity for pupils to recall their previous knowledge about the points of the compass and to acquire an understanding of bearings. Over-emphasis on the accuracy of angle measurements should be avoided at this stage.

Rescued from the sea

This situation provides a context within which pupils can practise and consolidate their newly acquired skills and concepts. The final task provides an opportunity for pupils to communicate to others about what they have learned.

Bird Island

This activity links work using coordinates with bearings, within a situation which is designed to arouse pupils' interest. Again, the final task provides an opportunity for pupils to communicate to others about what they have learned.

3-D coordinates

This situation links an everyday situation with the concepts of coordinates in three dimensions. Because pupils will be able to identify the relevance of the topic this should provide a high level of motivation.

3-D noughts and crosses

Playing the game is intended to reinforce and consolidate the work covered in this section.

. . . Directions

Answers

Page 44

1. North   2. 3 km   3. East   4. 030°, 4 km

5. From Westbury to Alton 000°; to Bedale 090°; to Caulton 030°; to Dalbry 080°; to Easton 210°; to Fenton 300°; to Granby 130°; to Highton 280°

6. To Westbury from Alton 180°; from Bedale 270°; from Caulton 210°; from Dalbry 260°; from Easton 030°; from Fenton 120°; from Granby 310°; from Highton 100°

7. From Westbury to Alton 3 km; to Bedale 5 km; to Caulton 4 km; to Dalbry 3 km; to Easton 2 km; to Fenton 5 km; to Granby 3 km; to Highton 4 km.

Page 45

1. Route B: 140°, 070°   Route C: 110°, 065°, 210°
2. Route B: 5 km, 2 km   Route C: 4 km, 3 km, 6 km

Page 46

1. Atlas 030°, Beatrice 240°
2. Atlas 25 km, Beatrice 30 km

Page 47

3. Heliport to Cleopatra 315°; Cleopatra to heliport 135°
4. Cleopatra to heliport 90 km
5. Rescue base to Cleopatra 070°; Cleopatra to Rescue base 250°
6. Rescue base to Cleopatra 35 km
7. Hospital to heliport 190°, 110°, 240°
8. 10 km, 50 km, 40 km
9. Heliport to hospital 060°, 290°, 010°
10. Heliport to hospital 40 km, 50 km, 10 km
11. Hospital to Base 190°, 110°, 240°, 270°, 340°, 260°, 320°
12. Hospital to Base 10 km, 50 km, 60 km, 40 km, 20 km, 20 km, 40 km
13. From Base to Hospital 140°, 080°, 160°, 090°, 060°, 290°, 010°
14. From Base to Hospital 40 km, 20 km, 20 km, 40 km, 60 km, 50 km, 10 km

Y7/8 SHAPE AND SPACE EXTENSION

Pages 44–51

Page 49

1. 2. 3.
   Raven Heights 5 km east and 7 km north
   (5, 7); 6.5 km, 035°
   Swallow Cliff 6 km east and 1 km north
   (6, 1); 6 km, 081°
   Crow Wood 3 km east and 2 km south
   (3, −2); 3.6 km, 123°
   Kestrel Ledge 5 km east and 6 km south
   (5, −6); 8 km, 140°
   Pheasant Thicket 2 km west and 1 km south
   (−2, −1); 2.3 km, 243°
   Cuckoo Wood 3 km west and 4 km north
   (−3, 4); 5 km, 323°
   Jackdaw Quarry 5 km west and 7 km north
   (−5, 7); 8.6 km, 325°

4. One strategy for keeping the journey short is to move in a clockwise direction.

Page 50

1. 9 C level 3, 11 C level 3
2. 10 C level 2, 10 C level 1
3. 4 B, 4 C, 5 B, 5 C; 18 B, 18 C, 19 B, 19 C
4. 320 spaces
5. Some possible situations include flats, aeroplanes, shipwrecks, oilfields.

Page 51

1. (0, 0, 2)
2. (0, 0, 0); (1, 1, 0); (2, 2, 0) or any other with the z coordinate a constant and the (x, y) coordinates on a straight line
3. (0, 0, 0); (0, 0, 1); (0, 0, 2), etc.
4. Any diagonal will do, e.g. (0, 0, 0); (1, 1, 1); (2, 2, 2)

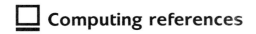 **Enlargement**

Activities

Fido	page 52
Rufus	page 53
Similarity	pages 53 – 55
Similar shapes	page 56
Enlarging maps	page 57
Rep-tiles	pages 58 – 59

Materials required

Computing references

Fido and Rufus

L Possible use of Logo
See **LP** R1, R2, V1, V2.

Links with National Curriculum Attainment Targets: Programmes of Study level descriptors

Teaching suggestions

This unit is designed to provide opportunities for pupils to acquire confidence in their ability to cope with situations in which they need to use and apply the concepts of scale factor and similarity.

Although pupils may benefit from working through some of these tasks on an individual basis, many of the activities are appropriate for small group work and opportunity for both pupil – pupil and teacher – pupil discussion should be provided.

It is desirable that pupils should complete this work using a calculator and that they should pool their ideas so that the tasks do not become onerous.

Fido and Rufus

These activities provide a gentle introduction to the concepts of similarity and scale factor. All the lines are straight and they are drawn on a square dotty grid.

Similarity

This task is more difficult because the leaves are on different orientations, lines are not straight and there is no grid. However, the leaves fall into two obvious categories. Within the two categories some leaves are similar but others are not.

Pupils should decide for themselves how they are going to decide which are similar. Perhaps they may decide to measure accurately the maximum lengths and widths of the leaves. This task and the next one, involving polygons, are group activities. They require pupils to adopt a methodical approach and to explain what they have tried to do.

The polygons fall into three categories: quadrilaterals, pentagons and decagons. Within each category some are similar. Pupils could be asked to measure the angles of the polygons as well as the lengths of the sides.

Similar shapes and Enlarging maps

These activities, which are related to real life, could be pursued on an individual basis to consolidate work already covered while working in a group.

Rep-tiles

This unit closes by providing a puzzle situation using the shape known as the sphinx which enables pupils to reflect on the concept of similarity.

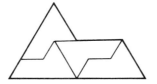

Sphinx made from four smaller rep-tiles

. . . **Enlargement**

Answers

Page 52

1. (Top) 17 mm, 7 mm, 12 mm
   (Bottom) 34 mm, 14 mm, 24 mm
2. (Top) 5 mm, 6 mm, 6 mm
   (Bottom) 10 mm, 12 mm, 12 mm
3. (Top) Eyes are 5 mm squares
   (Bottom) 10 mm squares
4. All measurements are 2 × original lengths.

Page 56

1. Check dimensions of house,
   e.g. Base   14 cm
          Roof height   10 cm
          Overall height   14 cm
2. Check dimensions of house,
   e.g. Base   3.5 cm
          Roof height   2.5 cm
          Overall height   3.5 cm

3.

	House A	House B	House C	Size B + Size A	Size C + Size A
Total height	7	14	3.5	2	0.5
Total width	7	14	3.5	2	0.5
Door height	2	4	1	2	0.5
Door width	1	2	0.5	2	0.5

Page 59

1.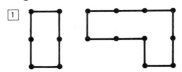

Unit 8 Pythagoras' theorem

Activities

Triangles from semi-circles pages 60–61

Finding areas by squaring   page 62

Using square-grid paper   page 63

The theorem of Pythagoras   page 64

Materials required

☐ Computing references

Pythagorean triples and Using Pythagoras' theorem

 Use of spreadsheet to investigate Pythagorean triples

Links with National Curriculum Attainment Targets: Programmes of Study level descriptors

NAT	Level	PoS Descriptor(s)
2	6	g
4	4	g
	7	c

Teaching suggestions

Triangles from semi-circles

This theorem is introduced here by means of a group activity. This involves the skills of drawing (semi-circles); of estimating measurements (of area); of deciding realistic units to use (of area); of presentation of results (in a table) and of making a conjecture about the results. This conjecture could be of the form 'It looks as if, when the largest angle is about 90°, the sum of the areas of the two smaller semi-circles is about the same as that of the larger semi-circle'.

This approach is used so that the pupils are not presented with the result to begin with but come to some understanding of it by experiment.

The resulting experience is wider than that usually given in two senses.

Firstly, the learner has laid down the foundations for the cosine rule, if he has made a conjecture about what happens in the cases when the largest angle is not 90°: 'If the largest angle is greater than 90°, then the area of the largest semi-circle is greater than the sum of the other two'.

Secondly, the results are true for any similar figures which are drawn on the sides of a triangle.

Finding areas by squaring

This activity repeats this approach, using squares, and gives more accurate results for the area by using a calculator. This should strengthen previous conjectures.

Using square grid paper

This activity uses the idea of dissections. Pupils should be familiar with this from their work on Tangrams. They can also use a 'subtraction' method by surrounding a shape whose area they wish to find by a larger shape whose area is easier to find.

The theorem of Pythagoras

Chinese proof, and Pythagoras' proof, use the dissection method.

To see this, pupils could be asked questions such as: What is the length of the side of the large square? What is the area of the triangle AED? What is the area of the square ABCD? What is the length of the side of this square (AD)?

Note that the statement of the theorem can be written in two ways, beginning 'The square on' or 'The square of'. 'On' emphasises the area aspects. 'Of' emphasises the numerical

The theorem of Pythagoras (continued)

aspect, and will lead on to Pythagorean triples in Shape and Space – Extension, Year 9. This could be introduced for abler pupils.

What sort of whole numbers will be sides of right-angled triangles? Can you use a spreadsheet to help you to do this? How would you use a calculator to help?

Answers

Page 63

1. 13 squares
2. White square: 1 square
   Red triangles: 3 squares each
3. 13 square cm

Page 65

1. 25 squares
2. 9 + 16 = 25 squares

Page 66

1. A square
2. Area = c^2
3. $c^2 = a^2 + b^2$

   $a^2 + b^2 = 2ab + x$
   where x is the area of the inside shape.
   $x = a^2 - 2ab + b^2 \equiv (a-b)^2$
   = a square of side $(a-b)$

Page 67

4.

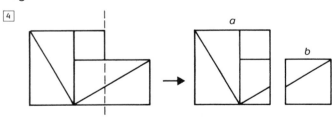

5. See ③ above for generalisation for basis.

Another method

1. A square
2. Area = c^2
3. Various acceptable methods.
4. Squares
5. b^2 and a^2
6. Pythagoras' or other methods.
7. By using all sides of the triangle in the methods described.

. . . **Pythagoras' theorem**

Page 69

1. 72 square cm

2. Measure as for a (3, 4, 5) triangle

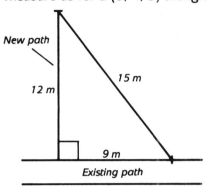

New path

12 m

15 m

9 m

Existing path

Use 27 m of tape as diagram.

3. $\sqrt{3}$

4. Any right-angled triangle where sides are

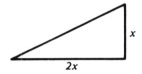

x

2x

Page 70

5. The perimeter of the square is made up from the hypotenuses of 12 triangles. The central body of the square will accommodate the remaining 48 triangles. There are other ways these can be arranged, our example, below, shows one way.

6. The square has the largest area.

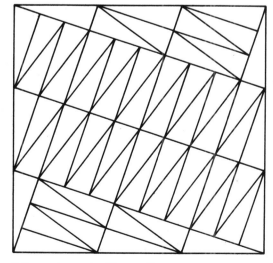

7. 3.5 m closer to the wall.

8. 8.5 squares

9. 17 squares

10. $\sqrt{108}$ cm

Unit 9 Moving points

Activities

Curves of loci	page 72
Linkages	pages 73–75
More investigations with linkages	pages 76–77
Curves from straight lines	page 78
Curves around you	page 79
People curves	pages 80–81
Curves of pursuit	pages 82–83

Materials required

Curves of loci and Linkages

 Materials for linkages:
Geostrips and paper fasteners or drinking straws and pipe cleaners or card strips, a hole punch and poppers

Curves around you

 String
Drawing pins

People curves

 Small objects such as blocks
Counters

💻 Computing references

Curves of loci, People curves and Curves of pursuit

 ATM Microworlds, 'Locus' and 'Multi-Logo'

Links with National Curriculum Attainment Targets: Programmes of Study level descriptors

NAT	Level	PoS Descriptor(s)
4	7	b

Teaching suggestions

Curves are discussed in this unit firstly as a locus – the path of a moving point which obeys a specific rule. Note that a locus need not be a complete curve. It could be a part of a curve, such as a semi-circle, or even a region, such as the interior of a circle. Discussion could enable pupils to invent rules which produce a locus of this type.

Secondly, curves are discussed as envelopes where the curve touches a set of moving lines which obey a specified rule. Pupils should be familiar with this aspect from curve stitching activities at Primary level. The book by Jon Millington, *Curve Stitching*, Tarquin Publications, 1989 contains many ideas, including computer program listings. Probably the earliest publication which deals with curve stitching is by Edith Somervell, *A rhythmic approach to mathematics*, which appeared in 1906 and is reprinted by the National Council of Teachers of Mathematics in the United States.

Linkages

Linkages are an efficient introduction to loci as pupils are enabled to make predictions as to what they expect to happen and then test them out in practice. Inadequate ideas are improved visually.

A curve formed from the three-strip linkage gives a good approximation to a straight line, for short distances. This is the locus of the midpoint of the middle strip. The complete locus is a figure of eight called the 'Lemniscate of Bernoulli'. The linkage was used by James Watt in his steam engine in about 1784. Other three-strip linkages are described in a book which may be available through inter-library loan: R.C. Yates, *Geometric Tools, a mathematical sketch and model book*, Educational Publishers, St. Louis, USA, 1949. Two other books of interest have been reprinted by the National Council of Teachers of Mathematics: A.B. Kempe, *How to draw a straight line*, Macmillan, 1877; and R.C. Yates, *Curves and their properties*, Edwards, Ann Arbor, Michigan, USA.

. . . Moving points

Answers

Page 80

1. A straight line – the perpendicular bisector

2.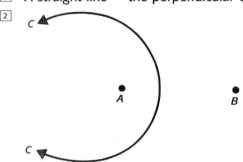

3. A semi-circle when 90° angle

Page 82

1.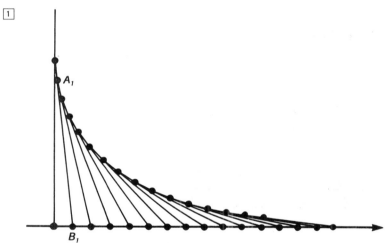

2. No
3. When she is directly behind Berinder.
4. Discuss the various ideas with the pupils.

Activities

Polyiamonds	page 84
Tessellating polyiamonds	page 85
Squares and rectangles	page 86
Designing tessellations	page 87
Curvy tiles	pages 88–89

Materials required

Squares and rectangles

 6

Square and rectangular tiles

Curvy tiles

◯ ATM tiles
Acetate sheet
OHP plus

💻 Computing references

Designing tessellations

L Use of Logo to help designing tessellations

Curvy tiles

L ATM Microworld 'Grids'

Links with National Curriculum Attainment Targets: Programmes of Study level descriptors

NAT	Level	PoS Descriptor(s)
4	4	b
	6	e

Teaching suggestions

The activities in this unit provide open-ended investigative tasks in which pupils can become involved as they consolidate their notions relating to the properties of polygons and the congruence of shapes.

Although pupils may benefit from working through some aspects of these tasks on an individual basis, many of the activities are appropriate for small group work. Opportunity for both pupil–pupil and teacher–pupil discussion should be provided at appropriate times during this work.

Polyiamonds, Tessellating polyiamonds, Squares and Rectangles, Designing tessellations and Curvy tiles

These activities require pupils to work systematically, record their results accurately, try all possible cases and detect congruent shapes. They also need to be able to explain their findings.

Answers

Page 84

1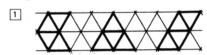

2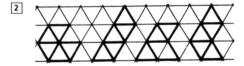

3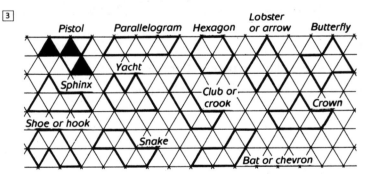

The 12 hexiamonds

Unit **11** Looking at solids

Activities

Isometric drawings	page 90
Optical illusions	page 91
Perspective drawing	pages 92–94
Drawing floor tiles and grids	page 95

Materials required

Computing references

L ATM Microworld 'Isogrid'

Links with National Curriculum Attainment Targets: Programmes of Study level descriptors

NAT	Level	PoS Descriptor(s)
4	6	a

Teaching suggestions

This unit is an extension of Unit 5, Making and drawing solids.

Isometric drawings

Isometric drawings are one way of showing pupils how to change from a two-dimensional to a three-dimensional perspective.

One possible approach to introducing pupils to isometric drawings is to ask them to close their eyes and 'visualise' a rectangle and rotate the rectangle so that they can 'see' the effect of rotation. This can be enhanced by many videos that look at rotating objects. Further development could be undertaken using the 'Isogrid' Microworld.

Optical illusions

This activity offers the pupils the opportunity to develop perspective through tessellation work. Pupils will find work that Escher has produced on tessellation stimulating and of interest. A useful source is the book by Bruner Ernst, *The Magic Mirror of M C Escher*, Tarquin Press, ISBN 0906212456. Further work relating to Escher can be found in the 'Patterns' Theme.

Perspective drawing

This activity affords pupils the opportunity of developing links with other areas of study, such as Technology and Art. A reference book edited by Leslie Jones, *The Teaching of Mathematics in Art*, Stanley Thornes (Publishers) Limited, 1991, will give pupils many further ideas to explore.

Answers

Page 94

1. The two outside posts are the same height.
2. The middle post
3. Only two outer ones are equal.
4.

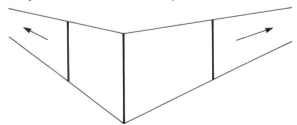

The drawing should show evidence of pupils taking the diagram off to the two vanishing points. Referencing these points on the shed diagram should be obvious.